DK

King Charles III

Celebrating His Majesty's Coronation and Reign

Written by Andrea Mills

Illustrated by Jennie Poh

DK | Penguin Random House

Editor Rona Skene
Consultant Dr. Carolyn Harris
Project Art Editors Charlotte Milner, Lucy Sims
Additional Design Ann Cannings, Sif Nørskov, Elle Ward
Jacket Designer Sif Nørskov
Publishing Assistant Rea Pikula
Managing Art Editor Diane Peyton Jones
Senior Production Editor Nikoleta Parasaki
Senior Production Controller Ena Matagic
Publisher Francesca Young
Publishing Director Sarah Larter

First American Edition, 2023
Published in the United States by DK Publishing
1745 Broadway, 20th Floor, New York, NY 10019

Copyright © 2023 Dorling Kindersley Limited
DK, a Division of Penguin Random House LLC
23 24 25 26 27 10 9 8 7 6 5 4 3 2 1
001–338096–May/2023

Published in Great Britain by Dorling Kindersley Limited

A catalog record for this book is available from the Library of Congress.
ISBN: 978-0-7440-8959-2

DK books are available at special discounts when purchased in bulk for
sales promotions, premiums, fund-raising, or educational use.
For details, contact: DK Publishing Special Markets,
1745 Broadway, 20th Floor, New York, NY 10019
SpecialSales@dk.com

Printed and bound in Slovakia

For the curious
www.dk.com

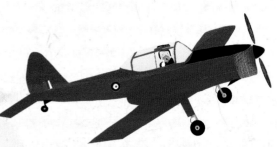

MIX
Paper | Supporting
responsible forestry
FSC™ C018179

This book was made with Forest Stewardship
Council™ certified paper – one small step in DK's
commitment to a sustainable future.
For more information go to
www.dk.com/our-green-pledge

Contents

A new King!

Please be upstanding for His Majesty, The King! In September 2022, King Charles III became the monarch of Britain and 14 other countries. The Coronation of the new King will be a day to celebrate!

Royal traditions

The Coronation ceremony follows centuries of tradition. The King will sit in King Edward's Chair, a throne made 700 years ago for Edward I. The St Edward's Crown will be placed on his head.

St Edward's Crown
This solid gold crown was made in 1661.

Coronation day

King Charles and Camilla, Queen Consort, will officially be crowned on 6 May 2023. The ceremony will take place almost exactly 70 years after the Coronation of The King's mother, Queen Elizabeth II.

It's a celebration!

The Coronation is a chance for everyone to celebrate. The ceremony in London will be attended by about 2,000 people, with thousands more lining the streets and millions worldwide watching on television.

Back to the day job

After the Coronation, the King will carry on with his daily duties, working with the UK government, and heading up a group of countries called the Commonwealth. The King also spends time on charity projects, plans royal tours, and attends special events. Phew – after all that it must be time for bed!

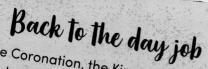

Famous face

His Majesty's face will be seen in lots of places! It will feature on all new British bank notes, coins, and stamps. The King's royal cypher, which is a crest created especially for him, will be used on UK government documents and on postboxes all over the country. The words "God Save the King!" will be sung at public events, as part of the National Anthem.

King Charles III
Buckingham Palace
London
United Kingdom

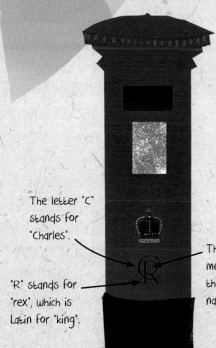

The letter "C" stands for "Charles".

"R" stands for "rex", which is Latin for "king".

The "III" means he is the third king named Charles.

Royal history

King Charles III takes his place in a long line of British kings and queens, dating back more than a thousand years.

Ancient rulers

For a long time, the United Kingdom (UK) didn't exist. Parts of the British Isles were ruled by different kings, queens, and chieftains. Over time, some areas joined up and became countries. Then in 1707, the UK was formed, made up of England, Wales, and Scotland. Later, Northern Ireland joined the UK, too.

Athelstan
925–939 CE

Grandson of Alfred the Great, Athelstan was the first king of all England. A successful military leader, he was also respected as a wise and fair ruler.

Harold I
1035–1040

Hardicanute
1040–1042

Canute
"The Great"
1016–1035

Edward
"The Confessor"
1042–1066

Edmund II
"Ironside"
1016

Harold II
1066

Sweyn
1013–1014

Aethelred II
"The Unready"
978–1013
1014–1016

Edward
"The Martyr"
975–978

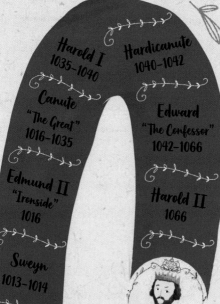

William I
"The Conqueror"
1066–1087

William, Duke of Normandy, invaded England with his army to claim the Crown. To defend his new kingdom, he built castles and forts all over the country.

Edgar
959–975

Eadwig
955–959

Eadred
946–955

Edmund I
939–946

William II
1087–1100

Henry I
1100–1135

Stephen
1135–1154

Henry II
1154–1189

Richard I
1189–1199

John
1199–1216

A real royal baddy, John is best known as the villainous king in the legend of Robin Hood. John pushed up taxes, fought costly wars, and was so unpopular that his subjects started a rebellion againt him!

Richard II
1377–1399

Edward III
1327–1377

Edward II
1307–1327

Edward I
1272–1307

Henry III
1216–1272

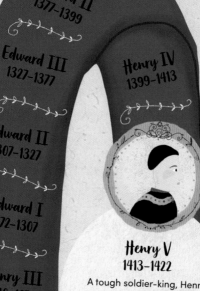

Henry V
1413–1422

A tough soldier-king, Henry went to war with France twice – and won! This popular monarch led his troops to victory at the Battle of Agincourt in 1415, inspiring William Shakespeare to write a play about him.

Henry IV
1399–1413

Henry VI
1422–1461
1470–1471

Edward IV
1461–1470
1471–1483

Edward V
1483

Edward VI
1547–1553

Mary I
1553–1558

George I
1714–1727

George II
1727–1760

Henry VIII
1509–1547

Crowned king as a teenager, Henry VIII ruled England for 38 years. After clashing with the Roman Catholic Church, he made himself head of his own Church of England. He is remembered most for marrying six times!

Elizabeth I
1558–1603

During Elizabeth's long reign, England became very rich and powerful. This was partly due to its strong navy, which defeated the Spanish fleet (Armada) in a fierce sea battle in 1588.

Anne
1702–1714

William III
1694–1702

William III Mary II
1689–1694

James II
1685–1688

George III
1760–1820

George IV
1820–1830

William IV
1830–1837

Modern monarchy

In centuries past, British monarchs had absolute power to create laws and make decisions. As a modern monarch, our King has a very different role. The government, which is voted for by the people, makes laws, then The King signs them to show his approval. Every week, he meets the Prime Minister to offer advice and guidance.

Henry VII
1485–1509

James I
1603–1625

Richard III
1483–1485

This monarch died while battling a rival for his crown. Then he resurfaced in 2012 when his remains were found beneath a car park in Leicester, England!

Charles I
1625–1649

The first King Charles was definitely not a popular monarch. He squabbled with his government and was eventually beheaded for treason. Ouch!

Charles II
1660–1685

Charles came to the throne after 11 years when there was no monarch. He was much more popular than his father, Charles I, and his cheerful personality led to him being nicknamed the Merry Monarch.

No monarch
1649–1660

Victoria
1837–1901

Queen Victoria's 63-year reign was a time of huge changes, sparked by new inventions and industries. Britain's power spread worldwide and by 1900, Her Majesty was Empress of 25 per cent of all the people on Earth!

Charles III
2022–today

Elizabeth II
1952–2022

George VI
1936–1952

Edward VIII
1936

Edward VII
1901–1910

George V
1910–1936

The King's lifetime

King Charles has lived a remarkable life on his way to becoming monarch. This timeline charts his story, including the events, occasions, and people that have had the most influence on him.

1948
Prince Charles, the first child of Princess Elizabeth and Prince Philip, is born at Buckingham Palace.

1952
Princess Elizabeth becomes Queen, making Prince Charles heir to the throne.

1 July 1969
The Queen invests her son as Prince of Wales in a ceremony at Caernarfon Castle in Wales.

12 July 1969
Prince Charles wins the Keyes Challenge Cup while playing polo for the President of Malta's team.

1970
The Prince studies history at Cambridge University and becomes the first heir to complete a university degree.

1971–1976
Prince Charles serves in the Royal Air Force, then joins the Royal Navy, captaining his own ship.

1984
Prince Charles and Princess Diana's second son, Prince Henry (Harry), is born.

1990
Duchy Originals, a food brand based on the produce grown on his estates, is set up by Prince Charles.

2005
Prince Charles marries for the second time. He and Camilla Parker-Bowles are married at the Windsor Guildhall.

2013
When Prince William and his wife Catherine have a baby boy, Prince George, Charles becomes a grandfather.

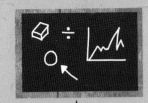

1953
The young Prince attends his mother's Coronation at Westminster Abbey.

1957
Prince Charles is the first royal heir to go to a school, rather than be educated at home.

1958
The Queen announces that she has bestowed the title "Prince of Wales" on 9-year-old Prince Charles.

1966
As part of a school exchange scheme, Prince Charles attends a grammar school in Australia.

1976
The Prince's Trust, a charity to support young, disadvantaged people, is set up by Prince Charles.

1980
The Prince moves to Highgrove House in Gloucestershire and sets up an organic farm there.

1981
The wedding of Charles and Lady Diana Spencer takes place at St Paul's Cathedral in London.

1982
Prince William is born, the first child of Prince Charles and Princess Diana.

2021
The Prince's father, Prince Philip, dies aged 99. He and Queen Elizabeth were married for 73 years.

2022
After a 70-year reign, Queen Elizabeth II dies on 7 September. Prince Charles is now King Charles III.

2023
The date of 6 May is set for The King's Coronation at Westminster Abbey in London.

The young Prince

Prince Charles made history from the moment he was born. As the future heir to the British throne, the news of his birth was reported all over the world. The Prince grew up with three younger siblings; his sister Princess Anne and two brothers, Princes Andrew and Edward.

Bundle of joy

Happy news came from Buckingham Palace on 14 November 1948. Princess Elizabeth and Prince Philip welcomed their first child, Charles Philip Arthur George, who was born in a guest room at the Palace. Everyone knew that one day, this newborn baby would become King.

Hyde Park, London

Spreading the news

News of the royal baby soon spread. The King's Troop Royal Horse Artillery fired a 41-gun salute: "BOOM!" The bells of Westminster Abbey chimed in celebration: "DING-DONG!" Newspaper front pages proclaimed the birth: "READ ALL ABOUT IT!"

Babies born in Britain on the same day as Prince Charles received a souvenir silver penny from the Royal Mint, Britain's official coin-makers.

By command of The Queen

The Earl Marshall is directed to invite

HIS ROYAL HIGHNESS PRINCE CHARLES

to the

CORONATION

on Tuesday June 2nd, 1953

Family ties

The family of King Charles is shown here as far back as Queen Victoria, his great-great-great grandmother. The King's grandfather, George VI, unexpectedly became monarch when his older brother, Edward VIII, announced that he could no longer be king, and gave up the throne.

Queen Victoria

Prince Albert

King Edward VII

Queen Alexandra

King Charles's royal relatives include the European monarchs King Harald V of Norway, Queen Margrethe II of Denmark, and King Felipe VI of Spain.

King George V

Queen Mary

King George VI

Queen Elizabeth

Personal invitation

When Charles was four years old, he received a very special, handmade invitation to attend the Coronation ceremony. Imagine! He was going to watch his mother be crowned Queen!

Queen Elizabeth II

Prince Philip

Coronation day

On 2 June 1953, The Queen's Coronation was held at Westminster Abbey in London. The ceremony lasted three hours, which was a long time for a four-year-old to sit still! Afterwards, Prince Charles stood with his mother on the balcony of Buckingham Palace and waved to the crowds. A noisy flypast of Royal Air Force planes was the highlight of his day!

King Charles III

Prince of Wales

When Prince Charles was 19 years old, he officially accepted the title of Prince of Wales, at a traditional ceremony called an investiture. More than 500 million people watched on television as the Prince received his new title from his mother, The Queen.

Castle ceremony

On 1 July 1969, the scene was set for the Prince to became Prince of Wales. Caernarfon Castle in Wales was the grand location for the open-air ceremony. About 4,000 guests crowded into the castle grounds to watch. Prince Charles kneeled on a cushion as The Queen handed him five royal objects, called insignia: a golden rod, a robe, a sword, a coronet (crown), and a ring.

"I, Charles, Prince of Wales, do become your liege man of life and limb and of earthly worship and faith and truth I will bear unto thee to live and die against all manner of folks."

Oath to The Queen taken by The Prince of Wales

Welsh traditions

Prince Charles's investiture ceremony was rooted in Welsh history. Caernarfon Castle was chosen because it was the birthplace of the first English Prince of Wales, Edward II, in 1284. Prince Charles gave some of his investiture speech in Welsh, after studying the language at university.

The story continues...

King Charles was Prince of Wales for a record-breaking 64 years until he became King. Soon after he came to the throne, The King announced that his son Prince William would follow in his footsteps by taking the title. Prince William and his wife Catherine were proclaimed the new Prince and Princess of Wales!

William and Catherine's wedding in 2011

Crowning moment

After The Queen placed the crown on her son's head and put the robe round his shoulders, she took his hands in hers. He was now officially Prince of Wales – a title only given to the British monarch's eldest son. The watching crowd cheered their new Prince of Wales. Hooray!

Flying high

As a young prince, Charles was a real-life action hero. His military career saw him take to the skies in the Royal Air Force and sail the oceans in the Royal Navy.

Learning to fly

Prince Charles first took flying lessons when he was at university. Then in 1971, he went to the Royal Air Force College. Under the name of Flight Lieutenant Wales, he was the first member of the Royal Family to gain his "wings" as a qualified jet-fighter pilot. He learned to fly helicopters, too. Chocks away!

The Prince learned to fly in a De Havilland Chipmunk, a small training plane.

Top ranks

The young Prince enjoyed his time in the military. After his retirement from service, he stayed involved with his naval and air force regiments. In 2012, The Queen bestowed on her son the highest ranks in all three armed services: Field Marshal of the British Army, Admiral of the Fleet in the Royal Navy, and Marshal of the Royal Air Force.

Field Marshal of the British Army

Admiral of the Fleet in the Royal Navy

Marshal of the Royal Air Force

The sky's the limit

Prince Charles tried skydiving for the first time in 1972, but his jump didn't go totally to plan! When the parachute opened, his legs became tangled in the rigging lines, so he found himself upside down as he floated downwards! Luckily, he still landed safely and was picked up from the ocean by his naval chums.

Like many sailors, Prince Charles was sometimes seasick in stormy seas. He has said that he often had to keep a bucket close by!

Life on the waves

In 1972, like his father, grandfather, and great-grandfathers before him, Prince Charles set sail with the Royal Navy. He learned the ropes on a ship called HMS *Norfolk* before being made captain of his own craft, HMS *Bronington*. The Prince's ship was a minesweeper, designed to find and destroy unexploded mines in the sea.

Fun and games

King Charles has always been a keen sportsman and has enjoyed playing many different sports. As well as becoming an expert polo player, he also loved skiing and scuba diving.

Polo star

Polo is a fast and furious sport that is a bit like hockey on horseback! The King first learned to play at school and he continued for more than 40 years. During that time, he was ranked in the top 10 of British players, and played for different teams all over the world.

Sport of kings

The King inherited a love of horses from his mother, Queen Elizabeth. In 1980, he rode his own horse, Allibar, in a steeplechase horse race in Ludlow, England, and came second! After the Queen's death in 2022, King Charles took over her stable of beloved racehorses.

Hitting the slopes

Skiing is one of The King's favourite sports. He has spent many holidays at his favourite resort, Klosters, in Switzerland, and took Princes William and Harry there to learn to ski, too. Once, in 1980, he put on a false moustache and big glasses, and told all the waiting photographers that Prince Charles would not be skiing that day!

Diving deep

During his time in the navy, Prince Charles tried scuba diving and loved it! He has explored under the ice in the Arctic Ocean, and made nine dives to the famous *Mary Rose* shipwreck off the English coast. The bad visibility underwater was described by him as "like diving in lentil soup"!

HRH
1

Football fan

The King loves the great outdoors, and goes hill-walking and fishing in the Scottish Highlands whenever he has time. His Majesty also enjoys watching football. He supports Burnley FC, where he has been given his own VIP season ticket.

The Prince's Trust

Back in 1976, Prince Charles set up his own small charity, The Prince's Trust. Today, the Trust is a worldwide success story, and has helped more than a million young people change their lives for the better.

Starting small

When Prince Charles left the Navy, he had a wonderful idea – to use the money he had earned as a naval officer to start a new charity. The Prince's Trust was set up to help young people aged between 11 and 30, who were struggling at school or finding it hard to get a job. The charity began by setting up small, local projects around the UK.

Famous faces

London youngsters Idris Elba and David Oyelowo were both given grants by The Prince's Trust to start training with the National Youth Theatre and the National Youth Music Theatre. Today they are both award-winning actors!

Idris Elba

David Oyelowo

Charity campaigners

Tim Peake

Many celebrities give time or money to the Trust. Astronaut Tim Peake raised funds by running a marathon from space! TV presenters Ant and Dec help young people find work in media. England men's football manager Gareth Southgate's scheme develops leadership skills. Rapper will.i.am's donation has helped young people train for careers in science and technology.

Ant and Dec

Gareth Southgate

will.i.am

Steps to success

The Trust really makes a difference! Three out of four young people who get involved with the charity move straight into work, education, or training. Free courses, grants, and mentoring give them both the confidence and the know-how to follow their dreams. Every year, their achievements are celebrated at a glittering awards ceremony.

Going global

In 2015, the charity went global with The Prince's Trust International, which has now spread into 17 countries across four continents. Thousands more young people have been able to change their lives, thanks to the training and support provided by the Trust.

Family man

Being King is a demanding job with lots of royal duties. King Charles spends any spare time he has with his family: Camilla, The Queen Consort, his two sons, five grandchildren, and five step-grandchildren.

Growing family

This family tree shows the King's two sons and their families. Prince William and his wife Catherine live in Windsor, England, with their three children. Prince Harry lives with his wife, Meghan, and their two children in California, USA. The King also has five step-grandchildren: Lola, Freddy, Eliza, Gus, and Louis.

Key

Marriage
Second marriage
Children

Lady Diana Spencer 1961–1997

King Charles III

Camilla Parker Bowles

Catherine Middleton

Prince William

Prince Harry

Meghan Markle

Prince George

Princess Charlotte

Prince Louis

Archie Mountbatten-Windsor

Lilibet Mountbatten-Windsor

Father and sons

Princes William and Harry followed in their father's footsteps and became skilled horsemen, talented polo players, and keen skiers. The young princes were taught to ride ponies by their father, in the grounds of Windsor Castle. The King also took part in Prince William's school sports day in 1989. He joined the other dads in a running race, and finished somewhere between first and last!

Proud grandpa

King Charles loves being a grandfather. On his public walkabouts, he often receives cards, toys, and gifts for his grandchildren from well-wishers. At Queen Elizabeth's Platinum Jubilee in 2022, The King had his hands full, keeping mischievous Prince Louis entertained on his lap as they watched the Jubilee pageant!

The King enjoys reading J.K. Rowling's *Harry Potter* books to his grandchildren, using different voices for the characters!

Festive treats

It was a family affair in 2019 when The Queen and the next three heirs to the throne gathered to make Christmas puddings for military veterans. Armed with wooden spoons, pudding bowls, and lucky sixpences, they had fun making the puddings together.

The Queen, Prince Charles, Prince William, and Prince George made the puddings at Buckingham Palace.

The green King

Today, many of us are concerned about challenges such as climate change, pollution, and endangered animals and plants. But King Charles was way ahead of his time. For years, he has been talking about green issues, and calling for us all to do our part to help sustain our planet.

Saving salmon

When he was young, Prince Charles noticed that there were fewer salmon in the rivers of the royal estates. He was so concerned that he wrote a letter to the UK Prime Minister, urging him to tackle the problem.

Planet in peril

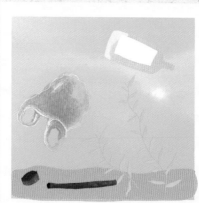

The Prince then focused on learning more about issues such as ocean pollution and endangered wildlife. He met many world leaders and campaigners to discuss ways to solve the problems.

On a trip to Borneo, Prince Charles made friends with an orang-utan in a rainforest!

Talking to trees

King Charles has always loved trees! He once told an interviewer that he talks to the trees in his garden because it helps them to grow. Science has since proved him right. The sound wave vibrations from talking really do make plants grow bigger and faster!

Wool is cool!

Every year, The King supports Wool Week, a celebration of all things woollen. As wool comes from sheep, it is more sustainable and uses fewer resources than many human-made fabrics.

Lasting legacy

The King's concern for the planet was shared by his father Prince Philip, who was president of the World Wildlife Fund. King Charles has passed on his passion to his sons, and in 2020, Prince William launched the **Earthshot Prize**. This scheme rewards people who find creative ways to tackle our urgent environmental problems.

A friend to animals

King Charles has visited the rainforests of Cameroon, spotted penguins in the South Atlantic, and had close encounters with lions on safari in Kenya. Back home, His Majesty is a big fan of red squirrels. At his estate in Scotland, he always keeps a stash of nuts in his pocket, so he can feed any squirrels he meets.

Home sweet home

Welcome to Highgrove House! King Charles has transformed his much-loved home from ordinary to organic. Wander around the house, gardens, and farm, but watch out for the free-range chickens!

House history

King Charles moved to Highgrove House in 1980 to get away from it all and enjoy the Cotswolds countryside. Princes William and Harry spent lots of time here as children, playing in the garden, riding their ponies, and setting up camp in the treehouse. Over the years, His Majesty has made many changes to the house and gardens to create his dream home.

The royal grandchildren measure their heights on this tree!

Eco-friendly home

Everything at Highgrove is designed to be green. Solar roof panels harness the power of the sun. In winter, the house is heated using wood-fuelled biomass boilers. Highgrove is also a chemical-free zone, using only natural cleaning products and fertilizers. Leftover food is recycled or made into compost to feed the flowers and vegetables.

Organic food brand

With his organic farm producing so much meat, vegetables, eggs, and honey, in 1990 Prince Charles set up a food company called Duchy Originals. Its range includes yummy biscuits, bread, fruit, herbs, and chutney. Profits go to The King's charities and raise more than £3 million every year.

Down on the farm

Next door to Highgrove is Home Farm, which grows organic crops and raises livestock. The farm has about 500 sheep, 200 cows, and 180 chickens that lay around 4,000 eggs every year. The chicken poo is collected and spread on the Highgrove flower and vegetable beds, as a natural fertilizer to help the plants grow.

Green-fingered King

With a wildflower meadow to attract bees and butterflies, plus a kitchen garden, sundial garden, and walled garden, there is always plenty of gardening to do! The flowers and vegetables are watered using rainwater and leftover bathwater.

The beehive is full of buzzy bees making delicious honey.

Buckingham Palace

Welcome to Royal Family headquarters! This palace in the heart of London attracts tourists from all over the world. It's full of history and has everything a modern monarch could wish for.

Palace past

When King George III bought the property in 1761, it was just a very big house! Work began to make it even bigger and grander. The first monarch to make it their offical home was Queen Victoria in 1837. Since then, four kings and one queen, Elizabeth II, have lived at Buckingham Palace.

Balcony view

On special occasions, the monarch and their family often stand on the giant balcony to wave to the people below. The balcony has also been the scene of several Royal-wedding kisses. Prince William and his new wife Catherine shared a smooch there in 2011, to the delight of the gathered crowd!

Fun facts

800 people work at the Palace.

Buckingham Palace and its gardens covers the same area as about **25** football pitches. That's seriously big!

The Palace has a total of **775** rooms, including **52** VIP bedrooms, **188** staff bedrooms, **78** bathrooms, **92** offices, and **19** State rooms.

In summer, the public can visit the **State Rooms** used for banquets and balls.

Royal announcements

When there is a birth or death in the Royal Family, a notice is placed on the front railings of the Palace. Everyone gathered outside can read the news and join in the celebrations or mourning.

Home comforts

When he is in London, The King works at Buckingham Palace but stays at nearby Clarence House, where he and The Queen Consort have lived for nearly 20 years. Sharing their home are two Jack Russell terriers called Beth and Bluebell. These lucky pooches were adopted by the Royal couple from Battersea Dogs and Cats Home in 2017.

Beth and Bluebell

Royal residences

The King has other official homes, including Windsor Castle in England, Hillsborough Castle in Northern Ireland, and the Palace of Holyroodhouse in Scotland. King Charles and his family have also spent many happy times at Balmoral Castle, their private holiday home in the Scottish Highlands.

Balmoral Castle

The Palace has a cinema, chapel, tennis court, swimming pool, post office, doctor's surgery, and cash machine!

The Palace has the **biggest private garden** in London.

Commonwealth leader

As well as being Britain's King, His Majesty's other job is leading the Commonwealth, a global family of countries. The members work together to help each other achieve their goals, overcome problems, and make life better for all their citizens.

Canada

The Bahamas
Belize
Jamaica
St Kitts and Nevis
Antigua and Barbuda
Dominica
Grenada
Saint Lucia
Barbados
St Vincent and the Grenadines
Trinidad and Tobago
Guyana

Commonwealth countries

This map shows all the countries in the Commonwealth. It began more than 100 years ago as a small group of countries – but has grown and grown. Today, there are 54 nations and territories with a total population of 2.5 billion people. As well as leading the Commonwealth, King Charles is king of 14 Commonwealth countries, including Jamaica, Canada, and Australia. The other member countries have their own monarchs or presidents.

Commonwealth Day is celebrated every year in March. Events are held all over the world to pay tribute to the friendship and unity within the Commonwealth family.

India, 2019

Jamaica, 2008

Seeing the world

King Charles is a real royal globetrotter and has visited most Commonwealth nations at least once. His Majesty regularly gets together with the leaders of Commonwealth countries to discuss the best ways to achieve their goals. He also meets visiting VIPs at the Commonwealth headquarters in London.

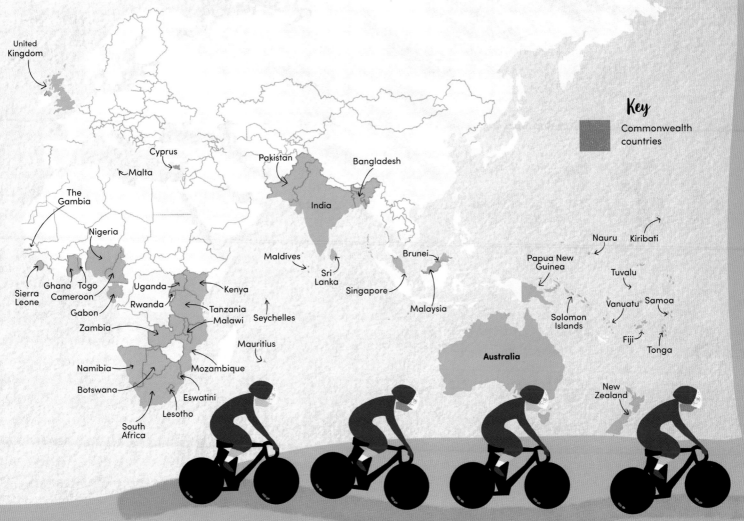

United Kingdom

Cyprus

Malta

The Gambia

Nigeria

Pakistan

Bangladesh

India

Sierra Leone

Ghana

Togo

Cameroon

Gabon

Uganda

Rwanda

Kenya

Tanzania

Malawi

Maldives

Sri Lanka

Singapore

Brunei

Malaysia

Nauru

Kiribati

Tuvalu

Papua New Guinea

Vanuatu

Samoa

Zambia

Seychelles

Mauritius

Solomon Islands

Fiji

Tonga

Namibia

Mozambique

Botswana

Eswatini

Lesotho

South Africa

Australia

New Zealand

Key

Commonwealth countries

The Queen started the baton relay for the 2022 Games!

Queen Elizabeth and athlete Kadeena Cox, 2021

Let the Games begin!

The Commonwealth Games is a huge, multi-sports event that takes place every four years. The 2022 Games were held in Birmingham, UK, and officially opened by Prince Charles. Before the Games in Australia in 2026, the King's Baton Relay will take place. A personal message from The King will be placed inside a baton, which will be carried by different people more than 145,000 km (90,000 miles) around all the Commonwealth countries. Wow!

Did you know?

You might think you know all there is to know about King Charles, but here are some fun facts about him that may surprise you...

One of The King's hobbies is painting landscapes in watercolours. He once sent a painting to the **Royal Academy** under the name "**Arthur George Carrick**" – and it was chosen for their annual exhibition!

As the monarch, King Charles is the only person in the UK who can travel abroad without a passport.

At tree-planting ceremonies, The King gives each tree a shake of its branches to wish it good luck!

Prince Charles made an appearance, as himself, in the long-running UK television drama **Coronation Street** in **2000**.

Prince Charles wrote a children's book entitled ***The Old Man of Lochnagar***, all about someone who lives in a Scottish cave. The tale was based on stories he shared with his younger siblings while they were growing up.

Rovers Return Inn